This book belongs to:

....

Table of Contents

Compiled by Dan Rude

Introduction

Ultimately, the goal of this study is to draw you near to God and be a tool to help you more fully comprehend who God is, what He has done for you, and how to live your new life to honor Him. As a Christian, one of the most important commitments you will ever make will be to faithfully read the Word of God.

Don't feel like each lesson needs to be done a certain way or completed in one sitting. Focus on what God is saying in each passage and how it applies to you. Give yourself time to process. Use these pages to connect with Him— whether that means journaling, drawing, writing a poem, or taking notes.

An important part of personal growth is community. Be intentional to pursue deeper conversations with your roommates, friends, family, and Community Group through this process. This study guide can be a place to collect your thoughts from sermons, Bible studies, and conversations with others.

Psalm 1:1-3

*1 How happy is the one who does not
walk in the advice of the wicked
or stand in the pathway with sinners
or sit in the company of mockers!
2 Instead, his delight is in the Lord's instruction,
and he meditates on it day and night.
3 He is like a tree planted beside flowing streams
that bears its fruit in its season
and whose leaf does not wither.
Whatever he does prospers.*

Unfortunately, few believers ever take the time to discover for themselves the life-changing truths contained in the Bible. But for those who do, it changes the whole direction of their lives, frees them from the power of sin, and helps them grow in their relationship with Jesus Christ.

Many believers have a desire to read the Word of God but aren't sure how to get started. This study guide is designed to encourage you to read the Bible, equip you to study it, and help you walk in obedience.

How to use this study

Below is an example of how to process through each section. There are many excellent ways to study the Bible—this is just a simple method that has been helpful to many people.

1. Try to get a feel for the context of the book.

Three basic questions that can help you understand the framework of the letter:
1. Who was the book written to?
2. Why was the book written? What problems are being dealt with?
3. How would the original audience have understood the text?

2. Read all the way through the passage.

2 Peter 1:3-9

3 His divine power has given us everything required for life and godliness through the knowledge of Him who called us by His own glory and goodness. 4 By these He has given us very great and precious promises, so that through them you may share in the divine nature, escaping the corruption that is in the world because of evil desires. 5 For this very reason, make every effort to supplement your faith with goodness, goodness with knowledge, 6 knowledge with self-control, self-control with endurance, endurance with godliness, 7 godliness with brotherly affection, and brotherly affection with love. 8 For if these qualities are yours and are increasing, they will keep you from being useless or unfruitful in the knowledge of our Lord Jesus Christ. 9 The person who lacks these things is blind and shortsighted and has forgotten the cleansing from his past sins.

3. Begin to write out what you observe.

Write down what initially stands out to you: truths about the character of God, the nature of man, nature of the world, sin, or things that make you think.

Observations

SAMPLE

v.3, God has given me everything I need for life and godliness, through the knowledge of God. God has given me what I need to do what He asks of me.

v.4, By His glory and goodness, He has given us great and precious promises.

v.4, God wants me to share in the divine nature. Whose divine nature? Not mine, but God's nature. God wants me to be like Him.

4. Identify the commands

Mark the passage with a "C" next to where the command begins. Some passages do not have commands, but if there are any commands, write out the command(s), and what you think it means.

Commands / what

SAMPLE

v.5-7, make every effort to supplement your faith with goodness, goodness with knowledge, 6 knowledge with self-control, self-control with endurance, endurance with godliness, 7 godliness with brotherly affection, and brotherly affection with love.

-There are 7 attributes God wants me to add to my faith.

5. Notice the reasoning

God wants us to understand not just what we believe, but why we believe what we believe. When we do, our convictions begin to grow. So ask the question: Why? Write out your responses and note any observations about the reasoning behind the passage.

Promises / why

SAMPLE

-Why should I obey v5 and make every effort to supplement my faith?

-v.8, The promise is that if I have these qualities and they are increasing, they will keep me from becoming useless and unfruitful in the knowledge of God.

6. Take note of principles

Look for any principles or general examples to follow.

Principles

SAMPLE

v.9, The reason we don't grow is that we are blind, nearsighted and have forgotten we have been forgiven from our past sins.

v.9, The growing Christian remembers his sins have been forgiven by Jesus. Forgotten here cannot mean deleted from memory all together. Forgotten has to mean he doesn't factor in the truth that he has been forgiven by the blood of Jesus Christ in the way he lives his life.

7. Find practical applications

Ask God, "What do you want me to take away from this passage?"

Practical Application

SAMPLE

- God has given my every thing I need to walk with Him. His promises help me experience His Divine nature. Therefore I need to do two things:

1. Make every effort (avoid being lazy) to add to my faith goodness, knowledge, etc.

2. Remember the truth that Jesus has forgiven my sins in the way I make my choices.

The Old Life

Genesis 3:1-21

1 Now the serpent was the most cunning of all the wild animals that the Lord God had made. He said to the woman, "Did God really say, 'You can't eat from any tree[a] in the garden'?"

2 The woman said to the serpent, "We may eat the fruit from the trees in the garden. 3 But about the fruit of the tree in the middle of the garden, God said, 'You must not eat it or touch it, or you will die.'"

4 "No! You will not die," the serpent said to the woman. 5 "In fact, God knows that when you eat it your eyes will be opened and you will be like God, knowing good and evil." 6 The woman saw[b] that the tree was good for food and delightful to look at, and that it was desirable for obtaining wisdom. So she took some of its fruit and ate it; she also gave some to her husband, who was with her, and he ate it. 7 Then the eyes of both of them were opened, and they knew they were naked[c]; so they sewed fig leaves together and made coverings for themselves.

8 Then the man and his wife heard the sound of the Lord God walking in the garden at the time of the evening breeze, and they hid from the Lord God among the trees of the garden. 9 So the Lord God called out to the man and said to him, "Where are you?"

10 And he said, "I heard you in the garden, and I was afraid because I was naked, so I hid."

11 Then he asked, "Who told you that you were naked? Did you eat from the tree that I commanded you not to eat from?"

12 The man replied, "The woman you gave to be with me—she gave me some fruit from the tree, and I ate."

13 So the Lord God asked the woman, "What is this you have done?" And the woman said, "The serpent deceived me, and I ate."

14 So the Lord God said to the serpent:

> Because you have done this, you are cursed more than any livestock and more than any wild animal. You will move on your belly and eat dust all the days of your life. 15 I will put hostility between you and

the woman, and between your offspring and her offspring. He will strike your head, and you will strike his heel.

16 He said to the woman:

I will intensify your labor pains; you will bear children with painful effort. Your desire will be for your husband, yet he will rule over you.

17 And he said to the man, "Because you listened to your wife and ate from the tree about which I commanded you, 'Do not eat from it':

The ground is cursed because of you. You will eat from it by means of painful labor all the days of your life. 18 It will produce thorns[d] and thistles for you, and you will eat the plants of the field. 19 You will eat bread by the sweat of your brow until you return to the ground, since you were taken from it. For you are dust, and you will return to dust." 20 The man named his wife Eve because she was the mother of all the living. 21 The Lord God made clothing from skins[e] for the man and his wife, and he clothed[f] them.

Notes

Cross references

a. Any tree

Genesis 2:16-17

16 And the Lord God commanded the man, "You are free to eat from any tree of the garden, 17 but you must not eat from the tree of the knowledge of good and evil, for on the day you eat from it, you will certainly die."

b. Saw

Psalm 73:1-3

1 Truly God is good to Israel, to those who are pure in heart. 2 But as for me, my feet had almost stumbled, my steps had nearly slipped. 3 For I was envious of the arrogant when I saw the prosperity of the wicked.

c. Naked

Genesis 2:23-25

23 And the man said:

This one, at last, is bone of my bone and flesh of my flesh; this one will be called "woman," for she was taken from man. 24 This is why a man leaves his father and mother and bonds with his wife, and they become one flesh. 25 Both the man and his wife were naked, yet felt no shame.

d. Thorns

John 19:1-6

1 Then Pilate took Jesus and had him flogged. 2 The soldiers also twisted together a crown of thorns, put it on his head, and clothed him in a purple robe. 3 And they kept coming up to him and saying, "Hail, King of the Jews!" and were slapping his face. 4 Pilate went outside again and said to them, "Look, I'm bringing him out to you to let you know I find no grounds for charging him." 5 Then Jesus came out wearing the crown of thorns and the purple robe. Pilate said to them, "Here is the man!" 6 When the chief priests and the temple servants saw him, they shouted, "Crucify! Crucify!" Pilate responded, "Take him and crucify him yourselves, since I find no grounds for charging him."

e. Skins

Romans 13:14

14 Rather, clothe yourselves with the Lord Jesus Christ, and do not think about how to gratify the desires of the flesh.

f. Clothed

John 1:29,35

29 The next day John saw Jesus coming toward him and said, "Here is the Lamb of God, who takes away the sin of the world!" 35 The next day, John was standing with two of his disciples.

Matthew 27:32-37

32 As they were going out, they found a Cyrenian man named Simon. They forced him to carry his cross. 33 When they came to a place called Golgotha (which means Place of the Skull), 34 they gave him wine mixed with gall to drink. But when he tasted it, he refused to drink it. 35 After crucifying him, they divided his clothes by casting lots. 36 Then they sat down and were guarding him there. 37 Above his head they put up the charge against him in writing: This Is Jesus, the King of the Jews.

Questions

What does this passage tell us about God?

What does this passage tell us about people?

How does this change how I see God?

How does this change how I treat other people?

What does God want me to know?

How does this passage change how I live?

Why does God want me to do these things?

Are there examples in this passage I can follow?

Notes

Prayer Requests

2

The New Life

John 3:1-21

1 There was a man from the Pharisees named Nicodemus, a ruler of the Jews. 2 This man came to him at night and said, "Rabbi, we know that you are a teacher who has come from God, for no one could perform these signs you do unless God were with him."

3 Jesus replied, "Truly I tell you, unless someone is born again, he cannot see the kingdom of God."

4 "How can anyone be born when he is old?" Nicodemus asked him. "Can he enter his mother's womb a second time and be born?"

5 Jesus answered, "Truly I tell you, unless someone is born of water and the Spirit[a], he cannot enter the kingdom of God. 6 Whatever is born of the flesh is flesh, and whatever is born of the Spirit is spirit. 7 Do not be amazed that I told you that you must be born again. 8 The wind blows where it pleases, and you hear its sound, but you don't know where it comes from or where it is going. So it is with everyone born of the Spirit."

9 "How can these things be?" asked Nicodemus.

10 "Are you a teacher of Israel and don't know these things?" Jesus replied. 11 "Truly I tell you, we speak what we know and we testify to what we have seen, but you do not accept our testimony. 12 If I have told you about earthly things and you don't believe, how will you believe if I tell you about heavenly things? 13 No one has ascended into heaven except the one who descended from heaven-the Son of Man[b].

14 "Just as Moses[c] lifted up the snake in the wilderness, so the Son of Man must be lifted up, 15 so that everyone who believes in him may have eternal life. 16 For God loved the world in this way: He gave his one and only Son, so that everyone who believes in him will not perish but have eternal life. 17 For God did not send his Son into the world to condemn the world, but to save the world through

him. 18 Anyone who believes in him is not condemned, but anyone who does not believe is already condemned, because he has not believed in the name of the one and only Son of God. 19 This is the judgment: The light has come into the world, and people loved darkness rather than the light because their deeds were evil. 20 For everyone who does evil hates the light and avoids it, so that his deeds may not be exposed. 21 But anyone who lives by the truth comes to the light, so that his works may be shown to be accomplished by God."

Notes

Cross references

a. Water and Spirit

Ezekiel 36:25-28

25 I will also sprinkle clean water on you, and you will be clean. I will cleanse you from all your impurities and all your idols. 26 I will give you a new heart and put a new spirit within you; I will remove your heart of stone and give you a heart of flesh. 27 I will place my Spirit within you and cause you to follow my statutes and carefully observe my ordinances. 28 You will live in the land that I gave your fathers; you will be my people, and I will be your God.

b. Son of Man

Daniel 7:9-14

9 As I kept watching, thrones were set in place, and the Ancient of Days took his seat. His clothing was white like snow, and the hair of his head like whitest wool. His throne was flaming fire; its wheels were blazing fire. 10 A river of fire was flowing, coming out from his presence. Thousands upon thousands served him; ten thousand times ten thousand stood before him. The court was convened, and the books were opened. 11 I watched, then, because of the sound of the arrogant words the horn was speaking. As I continued watching, the beast was killed and its body destroyed and given over to the burning fire. 12 As for the rest of the beasts, their dominion was removed, but an extension of life was granted to them for a certain period of time. 13 I continued watching in the night visions, and suddenly one like a son of man was coming with the clouds of heaven. He approached the Ancient of Days and was escorted before him. 14 He was given dominion, and glory, and a kingdom; so that those of every people, nation, and language should serve him. His dominion is an everlasting dominion that will not pass away, and his kingdom is one that will not be destroyed.

Matthew 26:62-68

62 The high priest stood up and said to him, "Don't you have an answer to what these men are testifying against you?" 63 But Jesus kept silent. The high priest said to him, "I charge you under oath by the living God: Tell us if you are the Messiah, the Son of God." 64 "You have said it," Jesus told him. "But I tell you, in the future you will see the Son of Man seated at the right hand of Power and coming on the clouds of heaven." 65 Then the high priest tore his robes and said, "He has blasphemed! Why do we still need witnesses? See, now you've heard the blasphemy. 66 What is your decision?" They answered, "He deserves death!" 67 Then they spat in his face and beat him; others slapped him 68 and said, "Prophesy to us, Messiah! Who was it that hit you?"

c. Moses

Numbers 21:4-9

4 Then they set out from Mount Hor by way of the Red Sea to bypass the land of Edom, but the people became impatient because of the journey. 5 The people spoke against God and Moses: "Why have you led us up from Egypt to die in the wilderness? There is no bread or water, and we detest this wretched food!" 6 Then the LORD sent poisonous snakes among the people, and they bit them so that many Israelites died. 7 The people then came to Moses and said, "We have sinned by speaking against the LORD and against you. Intercede with the LORD so that he will take the snakes away from us." And Moses interceded for the people. 8 Then the LORD said to Moses, "Make a snake image and mount it on a pole. When anyone who is bitten looks at it, he will recover." 9 So Moses made a bronze snake and mounted it on a pole. Whenever someone was bitten, and he looked at the bronze snake, he recovered

Questions

What does this passage tell us about God?

What does this passage tell us about people?

How does this change how I see God?

How does this change how I treat other people?

What does God want me to know?

How does this passage change how I live?

Why does God want me to do these things?

Are there examples in this passage I can follow?

Notes

Prayer Requests

3

The Satisfied Life / Part 1

John 4:1-26

1 When Jesus learned that the Pharisees had heard he was making and baptizing more disciples than John 2 (though Jesus himself was not baptizing, but his disciples were), 3 he left Judea and went again to Galilee. 4 He had to travel through Samaria; 5 so he came to a town of Samaria called Sychar near the property that Jacob had given his son Joseph. 6 Jacob's well was there, and Jesus, worn out from his journey, sat down at the well. It was about noon.

7 A woman of Samaria came to draw water.

"Give me a drink," Jesus said to her, 8 because his disciples had gone into town to buy food.

9 "How is it that you, a Jew, ask for a drink from me, a Samaritan woman?" she asked him. For Jews do not associate with Samaritans.

10 Jesus answered, "If you knew the gift[a] of God, and who is saying to you, 'Give me a drink,' you would ask him, and he would give you living water."

11 "Sir," said the woman, "you don't even have a bucket, and the well is deep. So where do you get this 'living water'[b]? 12 You aren't greater than our father Jacob, are you? He gave us the well and drank from it himself, as did his sons and livestock."

13 Jesus said, "Everyone who drinks from this water will get thirsty again. 14 But whoever drinks from the water that I will give him will never get thirsty again. In fact, the water I will give him will become a well of water springing up[c] in him for eternal life."

15 "Sir," the woman said to him, "give me this water so that I won't get thirsty and come here to draw water."

16 "Go call your husband," he told her, "and come back here."

17 "I don't have a husband," she answered.

"You have correctly said, 'I don't have a husband,'" Jesus said. 18 "For you've had five husbands, and the man you now have is not your husband. What you have said is true."

19 "Sir," the woman replied, "I see that you are a prophet. 20 Our fathers worshiped on this mountain, but you Jews say that the place to worship is in Jerusalem."

21 Jesus told her, "Believe me, woman, an hour is coming when you will worship the Father neither on this mountain nor in Jerusalem. 22 You Samaritans worship what you do not know. We worship what we do know, because salvation is from the Jews. 23 But an hour is coming, and is now here, when the true worshipers will worship the Father in Spirit and in truth. Yes, the Father wants such people to worship him. 24 God is spirit, and those who worship him must worship in Spirit and in truth."

25 The woman said to him, "I know that the Messiah is coming" (who is called Christ). "When he comes, he will explain everything to us."

26 Jesus told her, "I, the one speaking to you, am he."

Notes

Cross references

a. Gift

Romans 6:23

23 For the wages of sin is death, but the gift of God is eternal life in Christ Jesus our Lord.

John 4:14

14 But whoever drinks from the water that I will give him will never get thirsty again. In fact, the water I will give him will become a well of water springing up in him for eternal life.

b. Living Water

Jeremiah 2:9-13

9 Therefore, I will bring a case against you again. This is the Lord's declaration. I will bring a case against your children's children. 10 Cross over to the coasts of Cyprus and take a look. Send someone to Kedar and consider carefully; see if there has ever been anything like this: 11 Has a nation ever exchanged its gods? (But they were not gods!) Yet my people have exchanged their Glory for useless idols. 12 Be appalled at this, heavens; be shocked and utterly desolated! This is the Lord's declaration. 13 For my people have committed a double evil: They have abandoned me, the fountain of living water, and dug cisterns for themselves— cracked cisterns that cannot hold water.

c. Springing Up

John 7:37-39

37 On the last and most important day of the festival, Jesus stood up and cried out, "If anyone is thirsty, let him come to me and drink. 38 The one who believes in me, as the Scripture has said, will have streams of living water flow from deep within him." 39 He said this about the Spirit. Those who believed in Jesus were going to receive the Spirit, for the Spirit had not yet been given because Jesus had not yet been glorified.

Questions

What does this passage tell us about God?

What does this passage tell us about people?

How does this change how I see God?

How does this change how I treat other people?

What does God want me to know?

How does this passage change how I live?

Why does God want me to do these things?

Are there examples in this passage I can follow?

Notes

Prayer Requests

4

The Satisfied Life / Part 2

John 4:27-42

27 Just then his disciples arrived, and they were amazed that he was talking with a woman. Yet no one said, "What do you want?" or "Why are you talking with her?"

28 Then the woman left her water jar, went into town, and told the people, 29 "Come, see a man who told me everything I ever did. Could this be the Messiah?" 30 They left the town and made their way to him.

31 In the meantime the disciples kept urging him, "Rabbi, eat something."

32 But he said, "I have food to eat that you don't know about."

33 The disciples said to one another, "Could someone have brought him something to eat?"

34 "My food is to do the will of him who sent me and to finish his work," Jesus told them. 35 "Don't you say, 'There are still four more months, and then comes the harvest[a]'? Listen to what I'm telling you: Open your eyes and look at the fields, because they are ready for harvest. 36 The reaper is already receiving pay and gathering fruit for eternal life, so that the sower and reaper can rejoice together. 37 For in this case the saying is true: 'One sows[b] and another reaps.' 38 I sent you to reap what you didn't labor for; others have labored, and you have benefited from their labor."

39 Now many Samaritans from that town believed in him because of what the woman said when she testified, "He told me everything I ever did." 40 So when the Samaritans came to him, they asked him to stay with them, and he stayed there two days. 41 Many more believed because of what he said. 42 And they told the woman, "We no longer believe because of what you said, since we have heard for ourselves and know that this really is the Savior of the world."

Notes

Cross references

a. Harvest

Matthew 9:35-38

35 Jesus continued going around to all the towns and villages, teaching in their synagogues, preaching the good news of the kingdom, and healing every disease and every sickness. 36 When he saw the crowds, he felt compassion for them, because they were distressed and dejected, like sheep without a shepherd. 37 Then he said to his disciples, "The harvest is abundant, but the workers are few. 38 Therefore, pray to the Lord of the harvest to send out workers into his harvest."

b. Sows

Mark 4:13-20

13 Then he said to them: "Don't you understand this parable? How then will you understand all of the parables? 14 The sower sows the word. 15 Some are like the word sown on the path. When they hear, immediately Satan comes and takes away the word sown in them. 16 And others are like seed sown on rocky ground. When they hear the word, immediately they receive it with joy. 17 But they have no root; they are short-lived. When distress or persecution comes because of the word, they immediately fall away. 18 Others are like seed sown among thorns; these are the ones who hear the word, 19 but the worries of this age, the deceitfulness of wealth, and the desires for other things enter in and choke the word, and it becomes unfruitful. 20 And those like seed sown on good ground hear the word, welcome it, and produce fruit thirty, sixty, and a hundred times what was sown."

Questions

What does this passage tell us about God?

What does this passage tell us about people?

How does this change how I see God?

How does this change how I treat other people?

What does God want me to know?

How does this passage change how I live?

Why does God want me to do these things?

Are there examples in this passage I can follow?

Prayer Requests

5

The Divine Life

2 Peter 1:1-11

Greeting

1 Simeon Peter, a servant and an apostle of Jesus Christ:

To those who have received a faith equal to ours through the righteousness of our God and Savior Jesus Christ.

2 May grace and peace be multiplied to you through the knowledge of God and of Jesus our Lord.

Growth in the Faith

3 His divine power[a] has given us everything required for life and godliness through the knowledge[b] of him who called us by his own glory and goodness. 4 By these he has given us very great and precious promises[c], so that through them you may share in the divine nature[d], escaping the corruption that is in the world because of evil desire. 5 For this very reason, make every effort to supplement your faith with goodness, goodness with knowledge, 6 knowledge with self-control, self-control with endurance, endurance with godliness, 7 godliness with brotherly affection, and brotherly affection with love. 8 For if you possess these qualities in increasing measure, they will keep you from being useless or unfruitful in the knowledge of our Lord Jesus Christ. 9 The person who lacks these things is blind and shortsighted and has forgotten the cleansing from his past sins. 10 Therefore, brothers and sisters, make every effort to confirm your calling and election, because if you do these things you will never stumble. 11 For in this way, entry into the eternal kingdom of our Lord and Savior Jesus Christ will be richly provided for you.

Notes

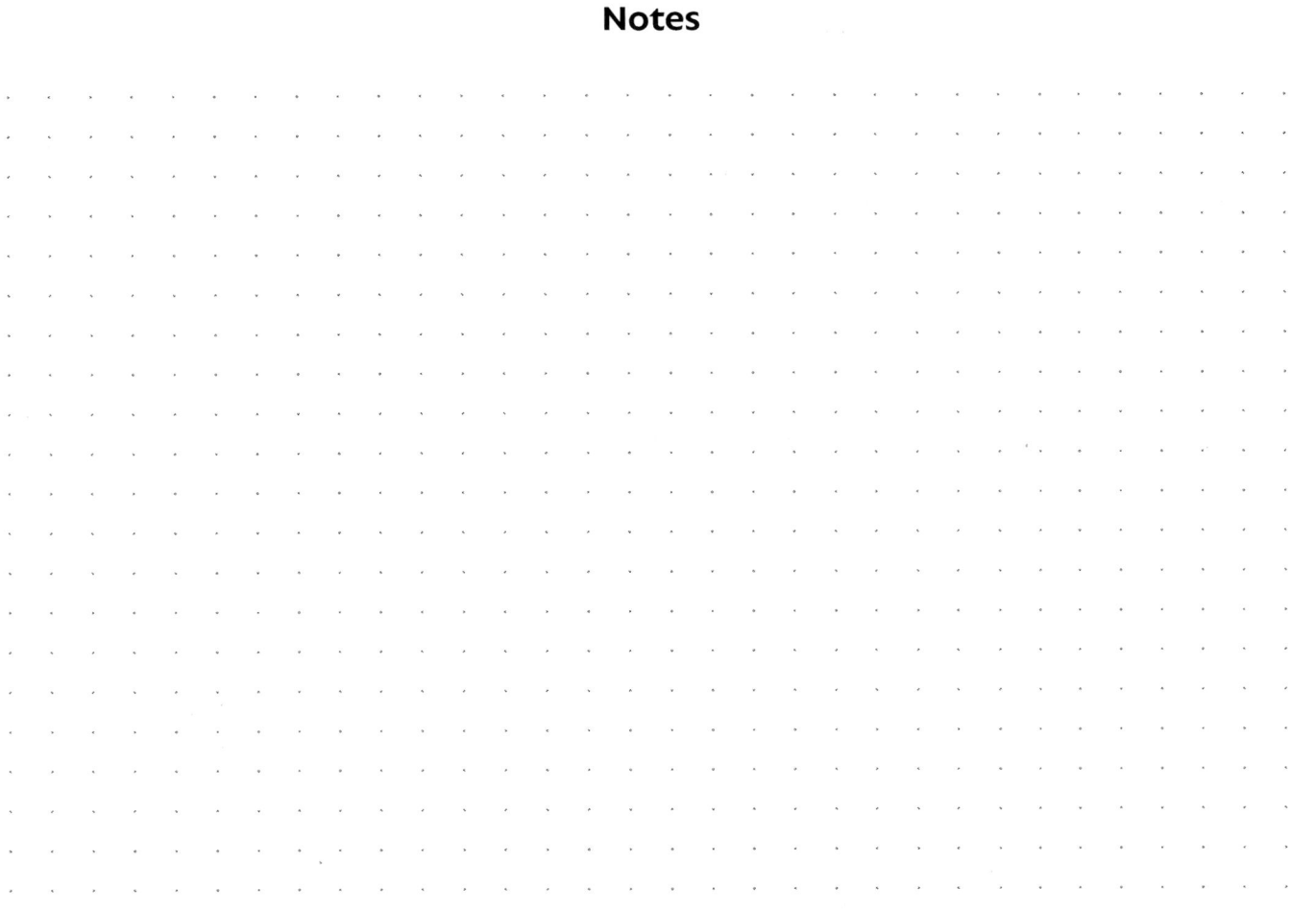

Cross references

a. Power

1 Peter 1:5

5 You are being guarded by God's power through faith for a salvation that is ready to be revealed in the last time.

b. Knowledge

John 17:3

3 This is eternal life: that they may know you, the only true God, and the one you have sent —Jesus Christ.

c. Promises

2 Corinthians 7:1

1 So then, dear friends, since we have these promises, let us cleanse ourselves from every impurity of the flesh and spirit, bringing holiness to completion in the fear of God.

d. Nature

Hebrews 12:10

10 For they disciplined us for a short time based on what seemed good to them, but he does it for our benefit, so that we can share his holiness.

Ephesians 4:24

24 and to put on the new self, the one created according to God's likeness in righteousness and purity of the truth.

Questions

What does this passage tell us about God?

What does this passage tell us about people?

How does this change how I see God?

How does this change how I treat other people?

What does God want me to know?

How does this passage change how I live?

Why does God want me to do these things?

Are there examples in this passage I can follow?

Prayer Requests

6

The Life of Faith / Part 1

Romans 4:1-25

1 What then will we say that Abraham, our forefather according to the flesh, has found? 2 If Abraham was justified by works, he has something to boast about—but not before God. 3 For what does the Scripture say? Abraham believed God, and it was credited to him for righteousness[a]. 4 Now to the one who works, pay is not credited as a gift, but as something owed. 5 But to the one who does not work, but believes on him who declares the ungodly to be righteous, his faith is credited for righteousness.

6 Just as David also speaks of the blessing of the person to whom God credits righteousness apart from works:

7 Blessed are those whose lawless acts are forgiven and whose sins are covered. 8 Blessed is the person the Lord will never charge with sin.

9 Is this blessing only for the circumcised, then? Or is it also for the uncircumcised[b]? For we say, Faith was credited to Abraham for righteousness. 10 In what way then was it credited—while he was circumcised, or uncircumcised? It was not while he was circumcised, but uncircumcised. 11 And he received the sign of circumcision as a seal of the righteousness that he had by faith while still uncircumcised. This was to make him the father of all who believe but are not circumcised, so that righteousness may be credited to them also. 12 And he became the father of the circumcised, who are not only circumcised but who also follow in the footsteps of the faith our father Abraham had while he was still uncircumcised.

13 For the promise to Abraham or to his descendants that he would inherit the world was not through the law, but through the righteousness that comes by faith. 14 If those who are of the law are heirs, faith is made empty and the promise nullified, 15 because the law produces wrath. And where there is no law, there is no transgression.

16 This is why the promise is by faith, so that it may be according to grace, to guarantee it to all the descendants—not only to those who are of the law but also to those who are of Abraham's faith. He is the father of us all. 17

As it is written: I have made you the father of many nations. He is our father in God's sight, in whom Abraham believed—the God who gives life to the dead and calls things into existence that do not exist. 18 He believed, hoping against hope, so that he became the father of many nations according to what had been spoken: So will your descendants be. 19 He did not weaken in faith when he considered his own body to be already dead (since he was about a hundred years old) and also the deadness of Sarah's womb. 20 He did not waver in unbelief at God's promise^c but was strengthened in his faith and gave glory to God, 21 because he was fully convinced that what God had promised, he was also able to do. 22 Therefore, it was credited to him for righteousness. 23 Now it was credited to him was not written for Abraham alone, 24 but also for us. It will be credited to us who believe in him who raised Jesus our Lord from the dead. 25 He was delivered up for our trespasses and raised for our justification.

Notes

Cross references

a. Righteousness

Genesis 15:6

6 Abram believed the Lord, and he credited it to him as righteousness.

b. Uncircumcised

Genesis 17:10-14

10 This is my covenant between me and you and your offspring after you, which you are to keep: Every one of your males must be circumcised. 11 You must circumcise the flesh of your foreskin to serve as a sign of the covenant between me and you. 12 Throughout your generations, every male among you is to be circumcised at eight days old—every male born in your household or purchased from any foreigner and not your offspring. 13 Whether born in your household or purchased, he must be circumcised. My covenant will be marked in your flesh as a permanent covenant. 14 If any male is not circumcised in the flesh of his foreskin, that man will be cut off from his people; he has broken my covenant.

c. Promise

2 Peter 1:3-4

3 His divine power has given us everything required for life and godliness through the knowledge of him who called us by his own glory and goodness. 4 By these he has given us very great and precious promises, so that through them you may share in the divine nature, escaping the corruption that is in the world because of evil desire.

Questions

What does this passage tell us about God?

What does this passage tell us about people?

How does this change how I see God?

How does this change how I treat other people?

What does God want me to know?

How does this passage change how I live?

Why does God want me to do these things?

Are there examples in this passage I can follow?

Notes

Prayer Requests

7

The Life of Faith / Part 2

Hebrews 11:1-11

1 Now faith is the reality of what is hoped for, the proof of what is not seen. 2 For by it our ancestors won God's approval.

3 By faith we understand that the universe was created by the word of God, so that what is seen was made from things that are not visible.

4 By faith Abel offered to God a better sacrifice than Cain did. By faith he was approved as a righteous man, because God approved his gifts, and even though he is dead, he still speaks through his faith.

5 By faith Enoch was taken away, and so he did not experience death. He was not to be found because God took him away. For before he was taken away, he was approved as one who pleased God. 6 Now without faith it is impossible to please God, since the one who draws near to him must believe that he exists and that he rewards[a] those who seek him.

7 By faith Noah[b], after he was warned about what was not yet seen and motivated by godly fear, built an ark to deliver his family. By faith he condemned the world and became an heir of the righteousness that comes by faith.

8 By faith Abraham, when he was called, obeyed and set out for a place that he was going to receive as an inheritance. He went out, even though he did not know where he was going. 9 By faith he stayed as a foreigner in the land of promise, living in tents as did Isaac and Jacob, coheirs of the same promise. 10 For he was looking forward to the city that has foundations, whose architect and builder is God.

11 By faith even Sarah herself, when she was unable to have children, received power to conceive offspring, even though she was past the age, since she considered that the one who had promised was faithful.

Notes

Cross references

a. **Rewards**

Hebrews 11:24-26

24 By faith Moses, when he had grown up, refused to be called the son of Pharaoh's daughter 25 and chose to suffer with the people of God rather than to enjoy the fleeting pleasure of sin. 26 For he considered reproach for the sake of Christ to be greater wealth than the treasures of Egypt, since he was looking ahead to the reward.

b. **Noah**

See Genesis 6:5-22

Questions

What does this passage tell us about God?

What does this passage tell us about people?

How does this change how I see God?

How does this change how I treat other people?

What does God want me to know?

How does this passage change how I live?

Why does God want me to do these things?

Are there examples in this passage I can follow?

Notes / Prayer Requests

The Spirit-filled Life

Galatians 5:16-26

16 I say then, walk[a] by the Spirit and you will certainly not carry out[b] the desire of the flesh. 17 For the flesh desires what is against the Spirit, and the Spirit desires what is against the flesh; these are opposed to each other, so that you don't do what you want. 18 But if you are led by the Spirit, you are not under the law.

19 Now the works of the flesh are obvious: sexual immorality, moral impurity, promiscuity, 20 idolatry, sorcery, hatreds, strife, jealousy, outbursts of anger, selfish ambitions, dissensions, factions, 21 envy, drunkenness, carousing, and anything similar. I am warning you about these things—as I warned you before—that those who practice such things will not inherit the kingdom of God.

22 But the fruit of the Spirit is love, joy, peace, patience, kindness, goodness, faithfulness, 23 gentleness, and self-control. The law is not against such things. 24 Now those who belong to Christ Jesus have crucified the flesh with its passions and desires. 25 If we live by the Spirit, let us also keep in step with the Spirit. 26 Let us not become conceited, provoking one another, envying one another.

Notes

Cross references

a. Walk

Ephesians 5:6-11, 15-21

6 Let no one deceive you with empty arguments, for God's wrath is coming on the disobedient because of these things. 7 Therefore, do not become their partners. 8 For you were once darkness, but now you are light in the Lord. Live as children of light— 9 for the fruit of the light consists of all goodness, righteousness, and truth— 10 testing what is pleasing to the Lord. 11 Don't participate in the fruitless works of darkness, but instead expose them. 15 Pay careful attention, then, to how you live—not as unwise people but as wise— 16 making the most of the time, because the days are evil. 17 So don't be foolish, but understand what the Lord's will is. 18 And don't get drunk with wine, which leads to reckless living, but be filled by the Spirit: 19 speaking to one another in psalms, hymns, and spiritual songs, singing and making music with your heart to the Lord, 20 giving thanks always for everything to God the Father in the name of our Lord Jesus Christ, 21 submitting to one another in the fear of Christ.

b. Carry Out

Romans 8:5-11

5 For those who live according to the flesh have their minds set on the things of the flesh, but those who live according to the Spirit have their minds set on the things of the Spirit. 6 Now the mind-set of the flesh is death, but the mind-set of the Spirit is life and peace. 7 The mind-set of the flesh is hostile to God because it does not submit to God's law. Indeed, it is unable to do so. 8 Those who are in the flesh cannot please God. 9 You, however, are not in the flesh, but in the Spirit, if indeed the Spirit of God lives in you. If anyone does not have the Spirit of Christ, he does not belong to him. 10 Now if Christ is in you, the body is dead because of sin, but the Spirit gives life because of righteousness. 11 And if the Spirit of him who raised Jesus from the dead lives in you, then he who raised Christ from the dead will also bring your mortal bodies to life through his Spirit who lives in you.

Questions

What does this passage tell us about God?

What does this passage tell us about people?

How does this change how I see God?

How does this change how I treat other people?

What does God want me to know?

How does this passage change how I live?

Why does God want me to do these things?

Are there examples in this passage I can follow?

Notes / Prayer Requests

The Life of Fellowship

Philippians 1:27-2:4

27 Just one thing: As citizens of heaven, live your life worthy of the gospel of Christ. Then, whether I come and see you or am absent, I will hear about you that you are standing firm in one spirit, in one[a] accord, contending together for the faith of the gospel, 28 not being frightened in any way by your opponents. This is a sign of destruction for them, but of your salvation—and this is from God. 29 For it has been granted to you on Christ's behalf not only to believe in him, but also to suffer for him, 30 since you are engaged in the same struggle that you saw I had and now hear that I have.

Christian Humility

1 If then there is any encouragement in Christ, if any consolation of love, if any fellowship with the Spirit, if any affection and mercy, 2 make my joy complete by thinking the same way, having the same love, united in spirit, intent on one purpose. 3 Do nothing out of selfish ambition or conceit, but in humility consider others as more important than yourselves. 4 Everyone should look out not only for his own interests, but also for the interests of others[b].

Notes

Cross references

a. One

John 17:20-23

20 I pray not only for these, but also for those who believe in me through their word. 21 May they all be one, as you, Father, are in me and I am in you. May they also be in us, so that the world may believe you sent me. 22 I have given them the glory you have given me, so that they may be one as we are one. 23 I am in them and you are in me, so that they may be made completely one, that the world may know you have sent me and have loved them as you have loved me.

b. Others

Hebrews 10:23-25

23 Let us hold on to the confession of our hope without wavering, since he who promised is faithful. 24 And let us watch out for one another to provoke love and good works, 25 not neglecting to gather together, as some are in the habit of doing, but encouraging each other, and all the more as you see the day approaching.

Hebrews 3:12-19

12 Watch out, brothers and sisters, so that there won't be in any of you an evil, unbelieving heart that turns away from the living God. 13 But encourage each other daily, while it is still called today, so that none of you is hardened by sin's deception. 14 For we have become participants in Christ if we hold firmly until the end the reality that we had at the start. 15 As it is said:

Today, if you hear his voice,

do not harden your hearts as in the rebellion.

16 For who heard and rebelled? Wasn't it all who came out of Egypt under Moses? 17 With whom was God angry for forty years? Wasn't it with those who sinned, whose bodies fell in the wilderness? 18 And to whom did he swear that they would not enter his rest, if not to those who disobeyed? 19 So we see that they were unable to enter because of unbelief.

Colossians 1:24-2:3

24 Now I rejoice in my sufferings for you, and I am completing in my flesh what is lacking in Christ's afflictions for his body, that is, the church. 25 I have become its servant, according to God's commission that was given to me for you, to make the word of God fully known, 26 the mystery hidden for ages and generations but now revealed to his saints. 27 God wanted to make known among the Gentiles the glorious wealth of this mystery, which is Christ in you, the hope of glory. 28 We proclaim him, warning and teaching everyone with all wisdom, so that we may present everyone mature in Christ. 29 I labor for this, striving with his strength that works powerfully in me.

1 For I want you to know how greatly I am struggling for you, for those in Laodicea, and for all who have not seen me in person. 2 I want their hearts to be encouraged and joined together in love, so that they may have all the riches of complete understanding and have the knowledge of God's mystery—Christ. 3 In him are hidden all the treasures of wisdom and knowledge.

Questions

What does this passage tell us about God?

What does this passage tell us about people?

How does this change how I see God?

How does this change how I treat other people?

What does God want me to know?

How does this passage change how I live?

Why does God want me to do these things?

Are there examples in this passage I can follow?

Notes / Prayer Requests

10

The Humble Life

John 13:1-38

1 Before the Passover Festival, Jesus knew that his hour[a] had come to depart from this world to the Father. Having loved his own who were in the world, he loved them to the end.

2 Now when it was time for supper, the devil had already put it into the heart of Judas, Simon Iscariot's son, to betray him. 3 Jesus knew that the Father had given everything into his hands, that he had come from God, and that he was going back to God. 4 So he got up from supper, laid aside his outer clothing, took a towel, and tied it around himself. 5 Next, he poured water into a basin and began to wash[b] his disciples' feet and to dry them with the towel tied around him.

6 He came to Simon Peter, who asked him, "Lord, are you going to wash my feet?"

7 Jesus answered him, "What I'm doing you don't realize now, but afterward you will understand."

8 "You will never wash my feet," Peter said.

Jesus replied, "If I don't wash you, you have no part with me."

9 Simon Peter said to him, "Lord, not only my feet, but also my hands and my head."

10 "One who has bathed," Jesus told him, "doesn't need to wash anything except his feet, but he is completely clean. You are clean, but not all of you." 11 For he knew who would betray him. This is why he said, "Not all of you are clean."

12 When Jesus had washed their feet and put on his outer clothing, he reclined again and said to them, "Do you know what I have done for you? 13 You call me Teacher and Lord—and you are speaking rightly, since that is what I am. 14 So if I, your Lord and Teacher, have washed your feet, you also ought to wash one another's feet. 15 For I have given you an example, that you also should do just as I have done for you.

16 "Truly I tell you, a servant is not greater than his master, and a messenger is not greater than the one who sent him. 17 If you know these things, you are blessed if you do them. 18 "I'm not speaking about all of you; I know those I have chosen. But the Scripture must be fulfilled: The one who

eats my bread has raised his heel against me. 19 I am telling you now before it happens, so that when it does happen you will believe that I am he. 20 Truly I tell you, whoever receives anyone I send receives me, and the one who receives me receives him who sent me."

21 When Jesus had said this, he was troubled in his spirit and testified, "Truly I tell you, one of you will betray me."

22 The disciples started looking at one another— uncertain which one he was speaking about. 23 One of his disciples, the one Jesus loved, was reclining close beside Jesus. 24 Simon Peter motioned to him to find out who it was he was talking about. 25 So he leaned back against Jesus and asked him, "Lord, who is it?"

26 Jesus replied, "He's the one I give the piece of bread to after I have dipped it." When he had dipped the bread, he gave it to Judas, Simon Iscariot's son. 27 After Judas ate the piece of bread, Satan entered him. So Jesus told him, "What you're doing, do quickly."

28 None of those reclining at the table knew why he said this to him. 29 Since Judas kept the money-bag, some thought that Jesus was telling him, "Buy what we need for the festival," or that he should give something to the poor. 30 After receiving the piece of bread, he immediately left. And it was night.

31 When he had left, Jesus said, "Now the Son of Man is glorified, and God is glorified in him. 32 If God is glorified in him, God will also glorify him in himself and will glorify him at once. 33 Children, I am with you a little while longer. You will look for me, and just as I told the Jews, so now I tell you: 'Where I am going, you cannot come.'

34 "I give you a new command: Love one another. Just as I have loved you, you are also to love one another. 35 By this everyone will know that you are my disciples, if you love one another."

36 "Lord," Simon Peter said to him, "where are you going?"

Jesus answered, "Where I am going you cannot follow me now, but you will follow later."

37 "Lord," Peter asked, "why can't I follow you now? I will lay down my life for you."

38 Jesus replied, "Will you lay down your life for me? Truly I tell you, a rooster will not crow until you have denied me three times.

Notes

Cross references

a. Hour

John 7:30

30 Then they tried to seize him. Yet no one laid a hand on him because his hour had not yet come.

John 8:20

20 He spoke these words by the treasury, while teaching in the temple. But no one seized him, because his hour had not yet come.

Mark 14:32-36

32 Then they came to a place named Gethsemane, and he told his disciples, "Sit here while I pray." 33 He took Peter, James, and John with him, and he began to be deeply distressed and troubled. 34 He said to them, "I am deeply grieved to the point of death. Remain here and stay awake." 35 He went a little farther, fell to the ground, and prayed that if it were possible, the hour might pass from him. 36 And he said, "Abba, Father! All things are possible for you. Take this cup away from me. Nevertheless, not what I will, but what you will."

Luke 22:42-45

42 "Father, if you are willing, take this cup away from me— nevertheless, not my will, but yours, be done." 43 Then an angel from heaven appeared to him, strengthening him. 44 Being in anguish, he prayed more fervently, and his sweat became like drops of blood falling to the ground. 45 When he got up from prayer and came to the disciples, he found them sleeping, exhausted from their grief.

b. Wash

Philippians 2:5-11

5 Adopt the same attitude as that of Christ Jesus, 6 who, existing in the form of God, did not consider equality with God as something to be exploited. 7 Instead he emptied himself by assuming the form of a servant, taking on the likeness of humanity. And when he had come as a man, 8 he humbled himself by becoming obedient to the point of death—even to death on a cross. 9 For this reason God highly exalted him and gave him the name that is above every name, 10 so that at the name of Jesus every knee will bow—in heaven and on earth and under the earth—11 and every tongue will confess that Jesus Christ is Lord, to the glory of God the Father.

Questions

What does this passage tell us about God?

What does this passage tell us about people?

How does this change how I see God?

How does this change how I treat other people?

What does God want me to know?

How does this passage change how I live?

Why does God want me to do these things?

Are there examples in this passage I can follow?

Notes

Prayer Requests

11

The Life of Prayer

Luke 11:1–13

1 He was praying in a certain place, and when he finished, one of his disciples said to him, "Lord, teach us to pray, just as John also taught his disciples."

2 He said to them, "Whenever you pray, say,

Father[a], your name be honored as holy. Your kingdom come. 3 Give us each day our daily bread.

4 And forgive us our sins, for we ourselves also forgive everyone in debt to us. And do not bring us into temptation."

5 He also said to them: "Suppose one of you has a friend and goes to him at midnight and says to him, 'Friend, lend me three loaves of bread, 6 because a friend of mine on a journey has come to me, and I don't have anything to offer him.' 7 Then he will answer from inside and say, 'Don't bother me! The door is already locked, and my children and I have gone to bed. I can't get up to give you anything.' 8 I tell you, even though he won't get up and give him anything because he is his friend, yet because of his friend's shameless boldness, he will get up and give him as much as he needs[b].

9 "So I say to you, ask[c], and it will be given to you. Seek, and you will find. Knock, and the door will be opened to you. 10 For everyone who asks receives, and the one who seeks finds, and to the one who knocks, the door will be opened. 11 What father among you, if his son asks for a fish, will give him a snake instead of a fish? 12 Or if he asks for an egg, will give him a scorpion? 13 If you then, who are evil, know how to give good gifts to your children, how much more will the heavenly Father give the Holy[d] Spirit to those who ask him?"

Notes

Cross references

a. Father

John 20:17

17 "Don't cling to me," Jesus told her, "since I have not yet ascended to the Father. But go to my brothers and tell them that I am ascending to my Father and your Father, to my God and your God."

1 Peter 1:17

17 If you appeal to the Father who judges impartially according to each one's work, you are to conduct yourselves in reverence during your time living as strangers.

b. Needs

Matthew 6:8

8 Don't be like them, because your Father knows the things you need before you ask him.

c. Ask

Matthew 6:5-8

5 Whenever you pray, you must not be like the hypocrites, because they love to pray standing in the synagogues and on the street corners to be seen by people. Truly I tell you, they have their reward. 6 But when you pray, go into your private room, shut your door, and pray to your Father who is in secret. And your Father who sees in secret will reward you. 7 When you pray, don't babble like the Gentiles, since they imagine they'll be heard for their many words. 8 Don't be like them, because your Father knows the things you need before you ask him.

d. Holy

John 1:33

33 I didn't know him, but he who sent me to baptize with water told me, 'The one you see the Spirit descending and resting on—he is the one who baptizes with the Holy Spirit.'

Questions

What does this passage tell us about God?

What does this passage tell us about people?

How does this change how I see God?

How does this change how I treat other people?

What does God want me to know?

How does this passage change how I live?

Why does God want me to do these things?

Are there examples in this passage I can follow?

Notes / Prayer Requests

12

The Generous Life

Matthew 6:19-34

19 "Don't store up for yourselves treasures on earth, where moth and rust destroy and where thieves break in and steal. 20 But store up for yourselves treasures[a] in heaven, where neither moth nor rust destroys, and where thieves don't break in and steal. 21 For where your treasure is, there your heart will be also.

22 "The eye is the lamp of the body. If your eye is healthy, your whole body will be full of light. 23 But if your eye is bad, your whole body will be full of darkness. So if the light within you is darkness, how deep is that darkness!

24 "No one can serve two masters[b], since either he will hate one and love the other, or he will be devoted to one and despise the other. You cannot serve both God and money.

25 "Therefore I tell you: Don't worry about your life, what you will eat or what you will drink; or about your body, what you will wear. Isn't life more than food and the body more than clothing? 26 Consider the birds of the sky: They don't sow or reap or gather into barns, yet your heavenly Father feeds them. Aren't you worth more than they? 27 Can any of you add one moment to his life span by worrying? 28 And why do you worry about clothes? Observe how the wildflowers of the field grow: They don't labor or spin thread. 29 Yet I tell you that not even Solomon in all his splendor was adorned like one of these. 30 If that's how God clothes the grass of the field, which is here today and thrown into the furnace tomorrow, won't he do much more for you—you of little faith? 31 So don't worry, saying, 'What will we eat?' or 'What will we drink?' or 'What will we wear?' 32 For the Gentiles eagerly seek all these things, and your heavenly Father knows that you need them. 33 But seek first the kingdom of God and his righteousness, and all these things will be provided for you. 34 Therefore don't worry about tomorrow, because tomorrow will worry about itself. Each day has enough trouble of its own.

Notes

Cross references

a. Treasures

Matthew 19:21

21 "If you want to be perfect," Jesus said to him, "go, sell your belongings and give to the poor, and you will have treasure in heaven. Then come, follow me."

b. Two Masters

Luke 16:13

13 No servant can serve two masters, since either he will hate one and love the other, or he will be devoted to one and despise the other. You cannot serve both God and money.

Hebrews 13:5

5 Keep your life free from the love of money. Be satisfied with what you have, for he himself has said, I will never leave you or abandon you

1 Timothy 6:6-8, 17-19

6 But godliness with contentment is great gain. 7 For we brought nothing into the world, and we can take nothing out. 8 If we have food and clothing, we will be content with these.

17 Instruct those who are rich in the present age not to be arrogant or to set their hope on the uncertainty of wealth, but on God, who richly provides us with all things to enjoy. 18 Instruct them to do what is good, to be rich in good works, to be generous and willing to share, 19 storing up treasure for themselves as a good foundation for the coming age, so that they may take hold of what is truly life.

Questions

What does this passage tell us about God?

What does this passage tell us about people?

How does this change how I see God?

How does this change how I treat other people?

What does God want me to know?

How does this passage change how I live?

Why does God want me to do these things?

Are there examples in this passage I can follow?

Notes / Prayer Requests

13

The Sexually Pure Life

1 Thessalonians 4:1-8

1 Additionally then, brothers and sisters, we ask and encourage you in the Lord Jesus, that as you have received instruction from us on how you should live and please God—as you are doing—do this even more. 2 For you know what commands we gave you through the Lord Jesus.

3 For this is God's will, your sanctification: that you keep away from sexual immorality, 4 that each of you knows how to control his own body in holiness and honor, 5 not with lustful[a] passions, like the Gentiles, who don't know God. 6 This means one must not transgress against and take advantage of a brother or sister in this manner, because the Lord is an avenger of all these offenses, as we also previously told and warned you. 7 For God has not called us to impurity but to live in holiness. 8 Consequently, anyone who rejects this does not reject man, but God, who gives you his Holy Spirit.

Notes

Cross references

a. **Lustful**

Matthew 5:27-30

27 You have heard that it was said, Do not commit adultery. 28 But I tell you, everyone who looks at a woman lustfully has already committed adultery with her in his heart. 29 If your right eye causes you to sin, gouge it out and throw it away. For it is better that you lose one of the parts of your body than for your whole body to be thrown into hell. 30 And if your right hand causes you to sin, cut it off and throw it away. For it is better that you lose one of the parts of your body than for your whole body to go into hell.

Questions

What does this passage tell us about God?

What does this passage tell us about people?

How does this change how I see God?

How does this change how I treat other people?

What does God want me to know?

How does this passage change how I live?

Why does God want me to do these things?

Are there examples in this passage I can follow?

Notes / Prayer Requests

The Thought Life

1 Peter 1:22-2:3

22 Since you have purified yourselves by your obedience to the truth, so that you show sincere brotherly love for each other, from a pure heart love one another constantly, 23 because you have been born again—not of perishable seed but of imperishable—through the living and enduring word of God. 24 For

> All flesh is like grass,
> and all its glory like a flower of the grass.
> The grass withers, and the flower falls,
> 25 but the word of the Lord endures forever.
> And this word is the gospel that was proclaimed[a]
> to you.

A Living Stone and A Holy People

1 Therefore, rid yourselves of all malice, all deceit, hypocrisy, envy, and all slander. 2 Like newborn infants, desire the pure milk of the word[b], so that you may grow up into your salvation, 3 if you have tasted that the Lord is good.

Notes

Cross references

a. Proclaimed

Mark 4:26-29

26 "The kingdom of God is like this," he said. "A man scatters seed on the ground. 27 He sleeps and rises night and day; the seed sprouts and grows, although he doesn't know how. 28 The soil produces a crop by itself—first the blade, then the head, and then the full grain on the head. 29 As soon as the crop is ready, he sends for the sickle, because the harvest has come."

b. Word

Romans 12:1-2

1 Therefore, brothers and sisters, in view of the mercies of God, I urge you to present your bodies as a living sacrifice, holy and pleasing to God; this is your true worship. 2 Do not be conformed to this age, but be transformed by the renewing of your mind, so that you may discern what is the good, pleasing, and perfect will of God.

Psalm 1:1-6

1 How happy is the one who does not walk in the advice of the wicked or stand in the pathway with sinners or sit in the company of mockers! 2 Instead, his delight is in the Lord's instruction, and he meditates on it day and night. 3 He is like a tree planted beside flowing streams that bears its fruit in its season and whose leaf does not wither. Whatever he does prospers.

4 The wicked are not like this; instead, they are like chaff that the wind blows away. 5 Therefore the wicked will not stand up in the judgment, nor sinners in the assembly of the righteous.

6 For the Lord watches over the way of the righteous, but the way of the wicked leads to ruin.

Psalm 119:9-11

9 How can a young man keep his way pure? By keeping your word. 10 I have sought you with all my heart; don't let me wander from your commands. 11 I have treasured your word in my heart so that I may not sin against you.

Ephesians 4:17-24

17 Therefore, I say this and testify in the Lord: You should no longer live as the Gentiles live, in the futility of their thoughts. 18 They are darkened in their understanding, excluded from the life of God, because of the ignorance that is in them and because of the hardness of their hearts. 19 They became callous and gave themselves over to promiscuity for the practice of every kind of impurity with a desire for more and more.

20 But that is not how you came to know Christ, 21 assuming you heard about him and were taught by him, as the truth is in Jesus, 22 to take off your former way of life, the old self that is corrupted by deceitful desires, 23 to be renewed in the spirit of your minds, 24 and to put on the new self, the one created according to God's likeness in righteousness and purity of the truth.

Questions

What does this passage tell us about God?

What does this passage tell us about people?

How does this change how I see God?

How does this change how I treat other people?

What does God want me to know?

How does this passage change how I live?

Why does God want me to do these things?

Are there examples in this passage I can follow?

Notes / Prayer Requests

15

The Justified Life

Romans 3:9-31

9 What then? Are we any better off? Not at all! For we have already charged that both Jews and Gentiles are all under sin, 10 as it is written:

There is no one righteous, not even one.

11 There is no one who understands;

there is no one who seeks God.

12 All have turned away;

all alike have become worthless.

There is no one who does what is good,

not even one.

13 Their throat is an open grave;

they deceive with their tongues.

Vipers' venom is under their lips.

14 Their mouth is full of cursing and bitterness.

15 Their feet are swift to shed blood;

16 ruin and wretchedness are in their paths,

17 and the path of peace they have not known.

18 There is no fear of God before their eyes.

19 Now we know that whatever the law[a] says, it speaks to those who are subject to the law, so that every mouth may be shut and the whole world may become subject to God's judgment. 20 For no one will be justified in his sight by the works of the law[b], because the knowledge of sin comes through the law.

21 But now, apart from the law, the righteousness of God has been revealed, attested by the Law and the Prophets. 22 The righteousness of God is through faith in Jesus Christ to all who believe, since there is no distinction. 23 For all have sinned and fall short of the glory of God. 24 They are justified freely by his grace through the redemption that is in Christ Jesus. 25 God presented him as an atoning sacrifice in his blood, received through faith, to demonstrate his righteousness, because in his restraint God passed over the sins previously committed. 26 God presented him to demonstrate his righteousness at the present time, so that he would be righteous and declare righteous the one who has faith in Jesus.

27 Where, then, is boasting? It is excluded. By what kind

of law? By one of works? No, on the contrary, by a law of faith. 28 For we conclude that a person is justified by faith apart from the works of the law. 29 Or is God the God of Jews only? Is he not the God of Gentiles too? Yes, of Gentiles too, 30 since there is one God who will justify the circumcised by faith and the uncircumcised through faith. 31 Do we then nullify the law through faith? Absolutely not! On the contrary, we uphold the law.

Notes

Cross references

a. Law

1 Timothy 1:8-9

8 But we know that the law is good, provided one uses it legitimately. 9 We know that the law is not meant for a righteous person, but for the lawless and rebellious, for the ungodly and sinful, for the unholy and irreverent, for those who kill their fathers and mothers, for murderers,

b. Law

Romans 10:2-4

2 I can testify about them that they have zeal for God, but not according to knowledge. 3 Since they are ignorant of the righteousness of God and attempted to establish their own righteousness, they have not submitted to God's righteousness. 4 For Christ is the end of the law for righteousness to everyone who believes.

Questions

What does this passage tell us about God?

What does this passage tell us about people?

How does this change how I see God?

How does this change how I treat other people?

What does God want me to know?

How does this passage change how I live?

Why does God want me to do these things?

Are there examples in this passage I can follow?

Notes

Prayer Requests

16

Life in the Vine

John 15:1-17

1 "I am the true vine[a], and my Father is the gardener. 2 Every branch in me that does not produce fruit he removes, and he prunes every branch that produces fruit so that it will produce more fruit[b]. 3 You are already clean because of the word I have spoken to you. 4 Remain in me, and I in you. Just as a branch is unable to produce fruit by itself unless it remains on the vine, neither can you unless you remain in me. 5 I am the vine; you are the branches. The one who remains in me and I in him produces much fruit, because you can do nothing without me. 6 If anyone does not remain in me, he is thrown aside like a branch and he withers. They gather them, throw them into the fire, and they are burned. 7 If you remain in me and my words remain in you, ask whatever you want and it will be done for you. 8 My Father is glorified by this: that you produce much fruit and prove to be my disciples.

9 "As the Father has loved me, I have also loved you. Remain in my love. 10 If you keep my commands you will remain in my love, just as I have kept my Father's commands and remain in his love.

11 "I have told you these things so that my joy[c] may be in you and your joy may be complete.

12 "This is my command: Love[d] one another as I have loved you. 13 No one has greater love than this: to lay down his life for his friends. 14 You are my friends if you do what I command you. 15 I do not call you servants anymore, because a servant doesn't know what his master is doing. I have called you friends, because I have made known to you everything I have heard from my Father. 16 You did not choose me, but I chose you. I appointed you to go and produce fruit and that your fruit should remain, so that whatever you ask the Father in my name, he will give you.

17 This is what I command you: Love one another."

Notes

Cross references

a. Vine

Isaiah 5:1-7

1 I will sing about the one I love, a song about my loved one's vineyard: The one I love had a vineyard on a very fertile hill. 2 He broke up the soil, cleared it of stones, and planted it with the finest vines. He built a tower in the middle of it and even dug out a winepress there. He expected it to yield good grapes, but it yielded worthless grapes. 3 So now, residents of Jerusalem and men of Judah, please judge between me and my vineyard. 4 What more could I have done for my vineyard than I did? Why, when I expected a yield of good grapes, did it yield worthless grapes? 5 Now I will tell you what I am about to do to my vineyard: I will remove its hedge, and it will be consumed; I will tear down its wall, and it will be trampled. 6 I will make it a wasteland. It will not be pruned or weeded; thorns and briers will grow up. I will also give orders to the clouds that rain should not fall on it. 7 For the vineyard of the Lord of Armies is the house of Israel, and the men of Judah, the plant he delighted in. He expected justice but saw injustice; he expected righteousness, but heard cries of despair.

b. Fruit

Galatians 5:22-23

22 But the fruit of the Spirit is love, joy, peace, patience, kindness, goodness, faithfulness, 23 gentleness, and self-control. The law is not against such things.

c. Joy

Psalm 4:7

7 You have put more joy in my heart than they have when their grain and new wine abound.

Psalm 16:11

11 You reveal the path of life to me; in your presence is abundant joy; at your right hand are eternal pleasures.

Psalm 32:2

2 How joyful is a person whom the Lord does not charge with iniquity and in whose spirit is no deceit!

Psalm 43:4

4 Then I will come to the altar of God, to God, my greatest joy. I will praise you with the lyre, God, my God.

Psalm 51:12

12 Restore the joy of your salvation to me, and sustain me by giving me a willing spirit.

d. Love

John 13:34-35

34 I give you a new command: Love one another. Just as I have loved you, you are also to love one another. 35 By this everyone will know that you are my disciples, if you love one another.

1 Peter 4:8

8 Above all, maintain constant love for one another, since love covers a multitude of sins.

Colossians 3:14

14 Above all, put on love, which is the perfect bond of unity.

Questions

What does this passage tell us about God?

What does this passage tell us about people?

How does this change how I see God?

How does this change how I treat other people?

What does God want me to know?

How does this passage change how I live?

Why does God want me to do these things?

Are there examples in this passage I can follow?

Notes / Prayer Requests

17

The Life of Endurance

Hebrews 12:1-13

1 Therefore, since we also have such a large cloud of witnesses surrounding us, let us lay aside every hindrance and the sin that so easily ensnares us. Let us run with endurance[a] the race that lies before us, 2 keeping our eyes on Jesus, the source and perfecter of our faith. For the joy[b] that lay before him, he endured the cross, despising the shame, and sat down at the right hand of the throne of God.

3 For consider him who endured such hostility[c] from sinners against himself, so that you won't grow weary and give up. 4 In struggling against sin, you have not yet resisted to the point of shedding your blood. 5 And you have forgotten the exhortation that addresses you as sons:

> My son, do not take the Lord's discipline lightly
> or lose heart when you are reproved by him,
> 6 for the Lord disciplines the one he loves
> and punishes every son he receives.

7 Endure suffering as discipline: God is dealing with you as sons. For what son is there that a father does not discipline? 8 But if you are without discipline—which all receive—then you are illegitimate children and not sons. 9 Furthermore, we had human fathers discipline us, and we respected them. Shouldn't we submit even more to the Father of spirits and live? 10 For they disciplined us for a short time based on what seemed good to them, but he does it for our benefit, so that we can share his holiness. 11 No discipline seems enjoyable at the time, but painful. Later on, however, it yields the peaceful fruit of righteousness to those who have been trained[d] by it.

12 Therefore, strengthen your tired hands and weakened knees, 13 and make straight paths for your feet, so that what is lame may not be dislocated but healed instead.

Notes

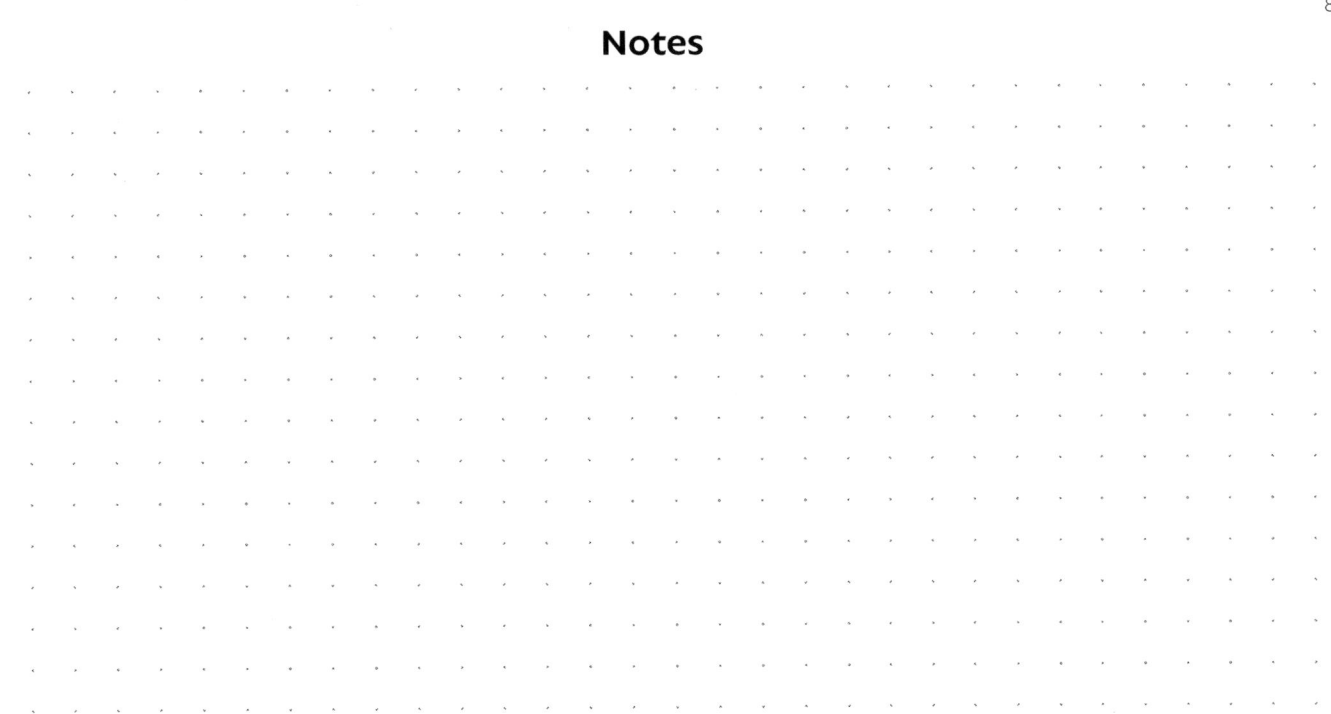

Cross references

a. Endurance

Hebrews 10:36

36 For you need endurance, so that after you have done God's will, you may receive what was promised.

James 1:2-4

2 Consider it a great joy, my brothers and sisters, whenever you experience various trials, 3 because you know that the testing of your faith produces endurance. 4 And let endurance have its full effect, so that you may be mature and complete, lacking nothing.

Romans 5:3-4

3 And not only that, but we also rejoice in our afflictions, because we know that affliction produces endurance, 4 endurance produces proven character, and proven character produces hope.

b. Joy

James 1:2

2 Consider it a great joy, my brothers and sisters, whenever you experience various trials.

c. Hostility

Mark 15:2-5

2 So Pilate asked him, "Are you the King of the Jews?"
He answered him, "You say so."

3 And the chief priests accused him of many things. 4 Pilate questioned him again, "Aren't you going to answer? Look how many things they are accusing you of!" 5 But Jesus still did not answer, and so Pilate was amazed.

d. Trained

Luke 6:40

40 A disciple is not above his teacher, but everyone who is fully trained will be like his teacher.

Hebrews 5:14

14 But solid food is for the mature—for those whose senses have been trained to distinguish between good and evil.

Questions

What does this passage tell us about God?

What does this passage tell us about people?

How does this change how I see God?

How does this change how I treat other people?

What does God want me to know?

How does this passage change how I live?

Why does God want me to do these things?

Are there examples in this passage I can follow?

Notes / Prayer Requests

18

The Intentional Life

1 Corinthians 9:19-27

19 Although I am free from all and not anyone's slave, I have made myself a slave to everyone, in order to win more people[a]. 20 To the Jews I became like a Jew, to win Jews; to those under the law, like one under the law—though I myself am not under the law—to win those under the law. 21 To those who are without the law, like one without the law—though I am not without God's law but under the law of Christ—to win those without the law. 22 To the weak I became weak, in order to win the weak. I have become all things to all people, so that I may by every possible means save some. 23 Now I do all this because of the gospel, so that I may share in the blessings.

24 Don't you know that the runners in a stadium all race, but only one receives the prize? Run in such a way to win the prize. 25 Now everyone who competes exercises self-control[b] in everything. They do it to receive a perishable crown, but we an imperishable crown[c]. 26 So I do not run like one who runs aimlessly or box like one beating the air. 27 Instead, I discipline my body and bring it under strict control, so that after preaching to others, I myself will not be disqualified.

Notes

Cross references

a. Win More People

Matthew 28:16-20

16 The eleven disciples traveled to Galilee, to the mountain where Jesus had directed them. 17 When they saw him, they worshiped, but some doubted. 18 Jesus came near and said to them, "All authority has been given to me in heaven and on earth. 19 Go, therefore, and make disciples of all nations, baptizing them in the name of the Father and of the Son and of the Holy Spirit, 20 teaching them to observe everything I have commanded you. And remember, I am with you always, to the end of the age."

Proverbs 11:30

11 The fruit of the righteous is a tree of life, and a wise person captivates people.

2 Corinthians 5:11

11 Therefore, since we know the fear of the Lord, we try to persuade people. What we are is plain to God, and I hope it is also plain to your consciences.

b. Self-Control

Acts 24:25

25 Now as he spoke about righteousness, self-control, and the judgment to come, Felix became afraid and replied, "Leave for now, but when I have an opportunity I'll call for you."

1 Corinthians 7:5

5 Do not deprive one another—except when you agree for a time, to devote yourselves to prayer. Then come together again, otherwise, Satan may tempt you because of your lack of self-control.

Galatians 5:22-23

22 But the fruit of the Spirit is love, joy, peace, patience, kindness, goodness, faithfulness, 23 gentleness, and self-control. The law is not against such things.

1 Thessalonians 5:6-8

6 So then, let us not sleep, like the rest, but let us stay awake and be self-controlled. 7 For those who sleep, sleep at night, and those who get drunk, get drunk at night. 8 But since we belong to the day, let us be self-controlled and put on the armor of faith and love, and a helmet of the hope of salvation.

2 Timothy 3:3, 4:5

3 unloving, irreconcilable, slanderers, without self-control, brutal, without love for what is good. 5 But as for you, exercise self-control in everything, endure hardship, do the work of an evangelist, fulfill your ministry.

c. Imperishable Crown

2 Corinthians 4:16-18

16 Therefore we do not give up. Even though our outer person is being destroyed, our inner person is being renewed day by day. 17 For our momentary light affliction is producing for us an absolutely incomparable eternal weight of glory. 18 So we do not focus on what is seen, but on what is unseen. For what is seen is temporary, but what is unseen is eternal.

Questions

What does this passage tell us about God?

What does this passage tell us about people?

How does this change how I see God?

How does this change how I treat other people?

What does God want me to know?

How does this passage change how I live?

Why does God want me to do these things?

Are there examples in this passage I can follow?

Notes / Prayer Requests

The Compassionate Life

Luke 10:25-37

25 Then an expert in the law stood up to test him, saying, "Teacher, what must I do to inherit eternal life?"

26 "What is written in the law?" he asked him. "How do you read it?"

27 He answered, "Love the Lord your God with all your heart, with all your soul, with all your strength, and with all your mind," and "your neighbor as yourself."

28 "You've answered correctly," he told him. "Do this and you will live."

29 But wanting to justify himself, he asked Jesus, "And who is my neighbor?"

30 Jesus took up the question and said: "A man was going down from Jerusalem to Jericho and fell into the hands of robbers. They stripped him, beat him up, and fled, leaving him half dead. 31 A priest[a] happened to be going down that road. When he saw him, he passed by on the other side. 32 In the same way, a Levite, when he arrived at the place and saw him, passed by on the other side. 33 But a Samaritan on his journey came up to him, and when he saw the man, he had compassion[b]. 34 He went over to him and bandaged his wounds, pouring on olive oil and wine. Then he put him on his own animal, brought him to an inn, and took care of him. 35 The next day he took out two denarii, gave them to the innkeeper, and said, 'Take care of him. When I come back I'll reimburse you for whatever extra you spend.'

36 "Which of these three do you think proved to be a neighbor to the man who fell into the hands of the robbers?"

37 "The one who showed mercy to him," he said.

Then Jesus told him, "Go and do the same."

Notes

Cross references

a. Priest

Matthew 5:43-48

43 You have heard that it was said, Love your neighbor and hate your enemy. 44 But I tell you, love your enemies and pray for those who persecute you, 45 so that you may be children of your Father in heaven. For he causes his sun to rise on the evil and the good, and sends rain on the righteous and the unrighteous. 46 For if you love those who love you, what reward will you have? Don't even the tax collectors do the same? 47 And if you greet only your brothers and sisters, what are you doing out of the ordinary? Don't even the Gentilesdo the same? 48 Be perfect, therefore, as your heavenly Father is perfect.

b. Compassion

Matthew 9:36

36 When he saw the crowds, he felt compassion for them, because they were distressed and dejected, like sheep without a shepherd.

Matthew 14:14

14 When he went ashore, he saw a large crowd, had compassion on them, and healed their sick.

Matthew 15:32

32 Jesus called his disciples and said, "I have compassion on the crowd, because they've already stayed with me three days and have nothing to eat. I don't want to send them away hungry, otherwise they might collapse on the way."

Mark 6:34

34 When he went ashore, he saw a large crowd and had compassion on them, because they were like sheep without a shepherd. Then he began to teach them many things.

Mark 8:2

2 I have compassion on the crowd, because they've already stayed with me three days and have nothing to eat.

Luke 1:78

78 Because of our God's merciful compassion, the dawn from on high will visit us.

Luke 15:20

20 So he got up and went to his father. But while the son was still a long way off, his father saw him and was filled with compassion. He ran, threw his arms around his neck, and kissed him.

1 Peter 3:8

8 Finally, all of you be like-minded and sympathetic, love one another, and be compassionate and humble.

1 John 3:17

17 If anyone has this world's goods and sees a fellow believer in need but withholds compassion from him—how does God's love reside in him?

Questions

What does this passage tell us about God?

What does this passage tell us about people?

How does this change how I see God?

How does this change how I treat other people?

What does God want me to know?

How does this passage change how I live?

Why does God want me to do these things?

Are there examples in this passage I can follow?

Notes/Prayer Requests

20

The Devoted Life

Mark 8:34-38

34 Calling the crowd[a] along with his disciples, he said to them, "If anyone wants to follow after me, let him deny himself, take up his cross, and follow me. 35 For whoever wants to save his life will lose it, but whoever loses his life because of me and the gospel will save it. 36 For what does it benefit someone to gain the whole world and yet lose his life? 37 What can anyone give in exchange for his life? 38 For whoever is ashamed of me and my words in this adulterous and sinful generation, the Son of Man will also be ashamed of him when he comes in the glory of his Father with the holy angels."

Notes

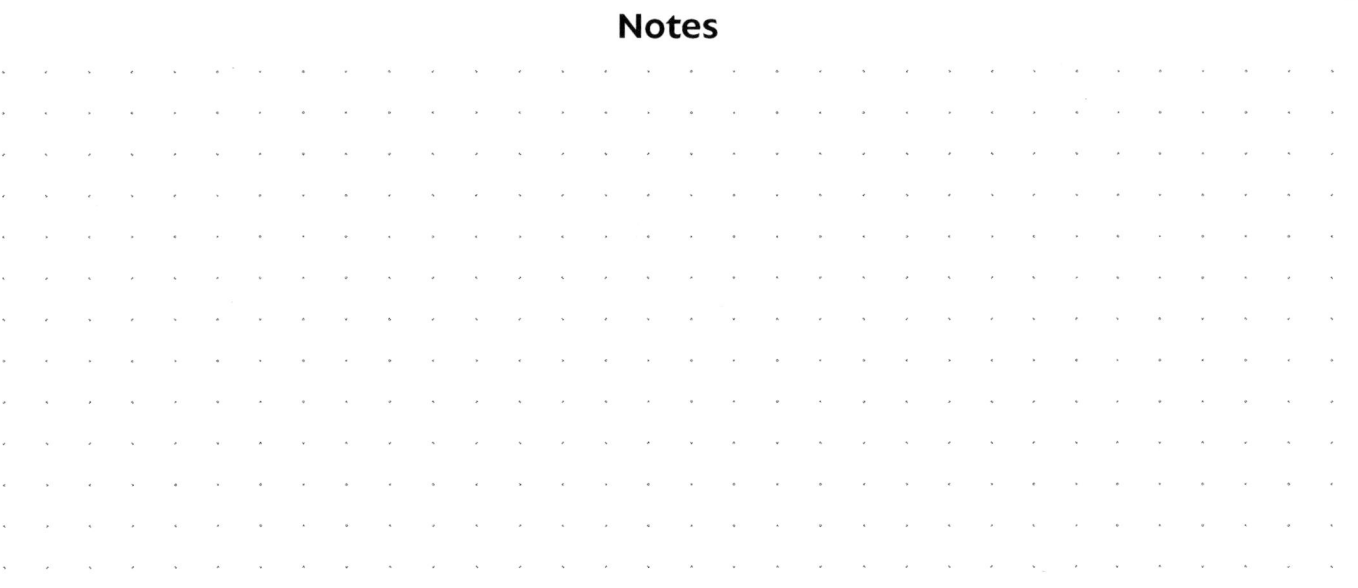

Cross references

a. Crowd

Luke 14:25-35

25 Now great crowds were traveling with him. So he turned and said to them: 26 "If anyone comes to me and does not hate his own father and mother, wife and children, brothers and sisters—yes, and even his own life—he cannot be my disciple. 27 Whoever does not bear his own cross and come after me cannot be my disciple.

28 "For which of you, wanting to build a tower, doesn't first sit down and calculate the cost to see if he has enough to complete it? 29 Otherwise, after he has laid the foundation and cannot finish it, all the onlookers will begin to ridicule him, 30 saying, 'This man started to build and wasn't able to finish.'

31 "Or what king, going to war against another king, will not first sit down and decide if he is able with ten thousand to oppose the one who comes against him with twenty thousand? 32 If not, while the other is still far off, he sends a delegation and asks for terms of peace. 33 In the same way, therefore, every one of you who does not renounce all his possessions cannot be my disciple.

34 "Now, salt is good, but if salt should lose its taste, how will it be made salty? 35 It isn't fit for the soil or for the manure pile; they throw it out. Let anyone who has ears to hear listen."

Questions

What does this passage tell us about God?

What does this passage tell us about people?

How does this change how I see God?

How does this change how I treat other people?

What does God want me to know?

How does this passage change how I live?

Why does God want me to do these things?

Are there examples in this passage I can follow?

Notes / Prayer Requests

Made in the USA
Columbia, SC
25 September 2020